Catholic Social Teaching:
13 Principles for Economic Policy

Written by

Father Matthew Nathan

Father Matthew Nathan Media

Bensenville, IL

2021

Catholic Social Teaching:
13 Principles for Economic Policy

Permissions
Cover photo: https://www.canva.com/media/MADaFoCNVWk
Cover and back design by April Stefanic

Nihil Obstat
Reverend John Balluff, S.T.D.
Censor Deputatus
September 22, 2021

Permission to Publish
Most Reverend Ronald A. Hicks
Bishop, Diocese of Joliet
October 7, 2021

TABLE OF CONTENTS

INTRODUCTION

Every one of us wants to see the world be a better place. For example, we all want to see fair work relations, an end to poverty, and everyone having an opportunity to maximize their potential. For all of this to happen, everyone in society needs to work together. That is where Catholic social teaching comes in.

WHAT IS CATHOLIC SOCIAL TEACHING?

Catholic social teaching refers to a set of Church teachings regarding modern societal issues like poverty, economics, labor, and international relations.

Its starting point is 1891, when Pope Leo XII wrote *Rerum Novarum*, literally the "new things" in society that came about because of the industrial changes in Europe during the nineteenth century. Many workers were exploited, so the pope decided to write moral guidelines about the "condition of labor," the subtitle of the pope's document.

Since then, popes have issued other documents about workers, political ideology, and national economic development as a response to the conditions of their time.

Even though there is no set list of Church documents that make up Catholic social teaching, the thirteen documents covered in this book are recognized as foundational. The following list shows the name of the document in Latin, its literal English translation in underlined italics, followed by the year it was published and lastly, the subtitle.

- *Rerum Novarum, <u>New Things</u>* (1891) On the Condition of Labor
- *Quadragesimo Anno, <u>40 Years</u>* (1931) On Reconstructing the Social Order
- *Mater et Magistra, <u>Mother and Teacher</u>* (1961) On Christianity and Social Progress
- *Pacem in Terris, <u>Peace on Earth</u>* (1963) On Peace among Peoples Based on Truth, Justice Charity, and Liberty
- *Gaudium et Spes, <u>Joy and Hope</u>* (1965) On the Church in the Modern World
- *Populorum Progressio, <u>Progress of Peoples</u>* (1967) On the Development of Peoples
- *Octogesima Adveniens, <u>Arrival of 80 Years</u>* (1971) On the Eightieth Anniversary of *Rerum Novarum*
- *Laborem Exercens, <u>Through Work</u>* (1981) On Human Work
- *Sollicitudo Rei Socialis, <u>Social Concern</u>* (1987) The Twentieth Anniversary of *Populorum Progressio*
- *Centesimus Annus, <u>100 Years</u>* (1991) The Hundredth Anniversary of *Rerum Novarum*
- *Caritas in Veritate, <u>Charity in Truth</u>* (2009) Integral Human Development in Charity and Truth
- *Laudato Si', <u>Praise Be to You</u>* (2015) On Care for Our Common Home
- *Fratelli tutti, <u>All Brothers</u>* (2020) On Fraternity and Social Friendship

Another way to look at these documents would be by the three different groupings shown in the following chart:

(1) *Rerum Novarum* and its sequels (the main theme being work relations). *Rerum Novarum* was such a landmark document that future popes also decided to write about work relations. These sequels, written on certain anniversaries of the encyclical, attempt to do what Pope Leo did in 1891: set out moral guidelines for fair work relations.

(2) *Populorum Progressio* and its sequels (on the development of nations). When Paul VI wrote *Populorum Progressio* in 1967, it inspired John Paul II and Benedict XVI to write sequels about what development should look like for all countries, in their respective time periods.

(3) Documents with no sequels (themes listed in parentheses).

(1) *Rerum Novarum* and its successors Theme: Work Relations	(2) *Populorum Progressio* and its successors Theme: The Development of Nations	(3) Documents with no successors Themes: In Parentheses
-Rerum Novarum -Quadragesimo Anno (40th anniversary) -Mater et Magistra (60th anniversary) -Octogesima Adveniens (80th anniversary) -Laborem Exercens (90th anniversary) -Centesimus Annus (100th anniversary)	-Populorum Progressio -Sollicitudo Rei Socialis (20th anniversary) -Caritas in Veritate (40th anniversary)	-Pacem in Terris (world peace) -Gaudium et Spes (role of the Church in the modern world) -Laudato Si' (environment) -Fratelli tutti (Globalization)

WHAT KIND OF DOCUMENTS ARE THESE?

There are different types of documents published by the Vatican. For example, there are papal homilies (when the pope reflects on Scriptures during mass), or liturgical directives (step-by-step guidelines on how to celebrate certain ceremonies). Twelve of the thirteen documents we'll look at are "encyclicals"—literally a "circular letter" that explains a certain part of our faith, designed for a worldwide audience. The one document here that isn't an encyclical is *Gaudium et Spes*, which is a "pastoral constitution"—a document that gives Catholics guidelines on how to live the Christian life. Links to all of these documents are in Appendix 1.

And now some good news and bad news about these foundational documents of Catholic social teaching. These documents offer incredible insight on how to apply the gospel to society and therefore make it better. But these documents are dense; combined with the fact that each document addresses multiple social issues, and it's easy to get overwhelmed.

In 2005, the Pontifical Council of Justice and Peace published the "Compendium of the Social Doctrine of the Church," which summarizes the important principals of Catholic social teaching. But the compendium is just as dense as the original documents—which is where this book comes in.

This book presents the documents of Catholic social teaching in chronological order and in an approachable way. This chronological presentation gives us an accurate idea of how Catholic social teaching developed over time, since each document builds on previous ones.

When presenting each document, I include the following:

The Historical Context: The occasion for the document, and societal trends at the time of the document's writing.

The Problem: Main issues unique to the time period of the document.

A Principle of Catholic Social Teaching: I emphasize "a" because I focus on one of the numerous principles each document has on how Catholics should approach economic realities. I've generally chosen a contribution that the document is either famous for promoting or a principle the document pays special attention to.

The Principle in Other Documents of Catholic Social Teaching (CST): Each principle will have explanation of how the principle has been articulated in other documents, including footnotes with substantive quotes. For each principle, I purposefully cite 7-8 different documents, primarily to show how these principles have been articulated by the Church over time. Furthermore, since the Catholic Church does not offer technical solutions to economic and social problems, a holistic view of these principles can make it easier for us to apply them.

For the "Problem" and "Principle" sections, I'll cite the paragraphs in the format they appear on the Vatican website (with paragraph number at the beginning of the citation). Also, I include some of the headings and section titles which are also helpful to understanding the text. I will use standard APA style citation for the footnotes, with full references at the end. Hopefully, by surrounding substantive CST texts with context and explanation, you'll find the entire corpus of CST less overwhelming.

I hope you enjoy this overview of Catholic social teaching, and that its insights will help you live our Catholic call to be great members of society.

1) *Rerum Novarum, <u>New Things</u>* (1891) On the Condition of Labor

Historical Context

As a result of the industrial revolution, manufacturers were taking advantage of workers' weak economic position by paying them low wages in dangerous working conditions.

Different political leaders and thinkers wanted to fix this situation. The most famous response came from Karl Marx, with his *Communist Manifesto* published in 1848. Although the Catholic Church understood Marxism's appeal, it condemned this philosophy because it explicitly rejected the spiritual nature of the human person and prioritized economic interest as the most important aspect of human existence.

However, Pope Leo XIII understood the injustices of the system and wrote *Rerum Novarum* to give orientation on how to interpret the new economic realities with the gospel.

The Problem

Workers (or "proletariat" as famously called in that era) were forced to move from rural areas to large cities since that was where all the jobs were. Factory owners could get away with providing bad wages and poor working conditions because (1) if an applicant said "no," that person didn't have any other income options to sustain himself and his family and (2) the employer could easily find someone else to hire because so many people were looking for work. Both of these circumstances created "utter poverty" for many working people.

> *3. Hence, by degrees it has come to pass that working men have been surrendered, isolated and helpless, to the hardheartedness of employers and the greed of unchecked competition. The mischief has been increased by rapacious usury, which, although more than once condemned by the Church, is nevertheless, under a different guise, but with like injustice, still practiced by covetous and grasping men. To this must be added that the hiring of labor and the conduct of trade are concentrated in the hands of comparatively few; so that a small number of very rich men have been able to lay*

upon the teeming masses of the laboring poor a yoke little better than that of slavery itself.

Most employers justified their actions by saying that when workers signed up for these jobs, they knew what they were getting into and freely agreed to the terms and conditions of work. Pope Leo recognized this argument and addressed it directly, saying that people who espoused this belief were leaving out the important factor of justice. This brings us to our first economic principle:

PRINCIPLE 1: JUST WORKING RELATIONS

Justice, not free agreement, should be the basis of all workplace relationships.

Free agreement isn't enough to make a work contract just. Sometimes, employers will exploit the weak position of a worker by offering bad pay in dangerous working conditions, making the agreement free but unjust. As Leo states:

> *45. If through necessity or fear of a worse evil the workman accept harder conditions because an employer or contractor will afford him no better, he is made the victim of force and injustice.*

JUST WORKING RELATIONS IN OTHER DOCUMENTS OF CST:

Unfortunately, Catholic social teaching has had to consistently speak out against the economically strong pressing their advantage against the economically weak. Pope John XXIII explicitly states that wages should not be left to the will of the more powerful[1], while Vatican II states that obedience to economic laws does not justify the detrimental treatment of workers[2]. Pope Benedict XVI emphasizes that societal

---

[1] We therefore consider it Our duty to reaffirm that the remuneration of work is not something that can be left to the laws of the marketplace; nor should it be a decision left to the will of the more powerful. It must be determined in accordance with justice and equity. (Mater et Magistra, para. 71)
[2] Any way of organizing and directing [economic activity] which may be detrimental to any working men and women would be wrong and

configurations and ideologies are what turn neutral economic instruments (like the free market) into forums where the strong subdue the weak[3].

Of course, the phrase "economically weak" has taken on a broader definition than exploited factory workers in 19th century England. For example, John Paul II reminds us that immigrant workers are consistently placed in vulnerable positions[4]. On an international level, Paul VI includes poorer nations trying to negotiate with wealthy ones as deserving protection against exploitation[5]. Similarly, John Paul II brings attention to the

---

inhuman. It happens too often, however, even in our days, that workers are reduced to the level of being slaves to their own work. This is by no means justified by the so-called economic laws. (Gaudium et Spes, para. 67)

[3] The Church has always held that economic action is not to be regarded as something opposed to society. In and of itself, the market is not, and must not become, the place where the strong subdue the weak. Society does not have to protect itself from the market, as if the development of the latter were *ipso facto* to entail the death of authentically human relations. Admittedly, the market can be a negative force, not because it is so by nature, but because a certain ideology can make it so. It must be remembered that the market does not exist in the pure state. It is shaped by the cultural configurations which define it and give it direction. (Caritas in Veritate, para. 36)

[4] The most important thing is that the person working away from his native land, whether as a permanent emigrant or as a seasonal worker, should not be *placed at a disadvantage* in comparison with the other workers in that society in the matter of working rights. Emigration in search of work must in no way become an opportunity for financial or social exploitation. As regards the work relationship, the same criteria should be applied to immigrant workers as to all other workers in the society concerned. The value of work should be measured by the same standard and not according to the difference in nationality, religion or race. (Laborem Exercens, para. 23)

[5] The teaching set forth by Our predecessor Leo XIII in *Rerum Novarum* is still valid today: when two parties are in very unequal positions, their mutual consent alone does not guarantee a fair contract; the rule of free consent remains subservient to the demands of the natural law. In *Rerum Novarum* this principle was set down with regard to a just wage for the individual worker; but it should be applied with equal force to contracts made between nations: trade relations can no longer be based solely on the principle of free, unchecked competition, for it very often creates an economic dictatorship. Free trade can be called just only when it conforms to the demands of social justice. (Populorum Progressio, para. 59)

practice wealthy nations reducing their production costs by contracting with poorer countries where labor exploitation is common[6].

The principle of just working relations is a fundamental starting point of Catholic social teaching, but not its ending point. As John Paul II said on the 100th anniversary of *Rerum Novarum*, just relationships in all areas of society (including in economics) serves as the foundation of peace[7]. One of the great contributions of *Rerum Novarum* is that it offered broad remedies to injustice, like union negotiations[8] or government intervention[9]. As we will soon see, Catholic social teaching has a number of other remedies to propose.

---

[6] There exists, too, a kind of international division of labor, whereby the low-cost products of certain countries which lack effective labor laws or which are too weak to apply them are sold in other parts of the world at considerable profit for the companies engaged in this form of production, which knows no frontiers. (Sollicitudo Rei Socialis, para. 43)
[7] However, the Pope [Leo XIII] was very much aware that *peace is built on the foundation of justice:* what was essential to the Encyclical [Rerum Novarum] was precisely its proclamation of the fundamental conditions for justice in the economic and social situation of the time. (Centesimus Annus, para. 5)
[8] It is gratifying to know that there are actually in existence not a few associations of this nature, consisting either of workmen alone, or of workmen and employers together, but it were greatly to be desired that they should become more numerous and more efficient. We have spoken of them more than once, yet it will be well to explain here how notably they are needed, to show that they exist of their own right, and what should be their organization and their mode of action. (Rerum Novarum, para. 49)
[9] Still, when there is question of defending the rights of individuals, the poor and badly off have a claim to especial consideration. The richer class have many ways of shielding themselves, and stand less in need of help from the State; whereas the mass of the poor have no resources of their own to fall back upon, and must chiefly depend upon the assistance of the State. And it is for this reason that wage-earners, since they mostly belong in the mass of the needy, should be specially cared for and protected by the government. (Rerum Novarum, para. 37)

2) *Quadragesimo Anno, 40 Years* (1931) On Reconstructing the Social Order

Historical Context

Rerum Novarum was wildly popular among rich and poor alike, since both classes accepted (in theory) the moral guidance it offered.

The encyclical's biggest influence was in encouraging workers to continue their free associations (unions). From a faith perspective, Catholic union members viewed their union negotiations as following Leo's call for just working relations, rather than following Marx's call to overthrow rich people in power.

Pope Pius XI wrote *Quadragesimo Anno* to commemorate the fortieth anniversary of *Rerum Novarum* and dedicates the first part of the encyclical celebrating its influence on society. In the rest of the encyclical, Pius applies its principles to the situation of his time, which was suffering from a worldwide economic depression that began in 1929.

The Problem

Despite *Rerum Novarum's* popularity, tension was still growing between rich and poor. Pius attributes this to three things: (1) companies, in their effort to gain "economic supremacy," still don't respect the rights of the worker; (2) many of these rich employers seek to use the government to create laws that maintain the current system they are benefitting from; and (3) richer countries exploit economically poorer countries.

> *108. This accumulation of might and of power generates in turn three kinds of conflict. First, there is the struggle for economic supremacy itself; then there is the bitter fight to gain supremacy over the State in order to use in economic struggles its resources and authority; finally there is conflict between States themselves, not only because countries employ their power and shape their policies to promote every economic advantage of their citizens, but also because they seek to decide political controversies that arise*

among nations through the use of their economic supremacy and strength.

Since so many individuals were still being treated badly by the more powerful, socialists proposed to have the national government intervene directly whenever civic disputes arose. However, Pope Pius reminds all parties involved that intermediary entities (unions, worker associations, local authorities) should be utilized to remedy a problem before seeking a solution from the national authorities. This brings us to our second economic principle:

PRINCIPLE 2: SUBSIDIARITY

The social entity closest to a problem should be the first one to try to solve it. If the problem is too big for them, then larger entities can intervene. The largest entity (the State), should not intervene prematurely or absorb the duties that correspond to the smaller entities.

> *79. Still, that most weighty principle, which cannot be set aside or changed, remains fixed and unshaken in social philosophy: Just as it is gravely wrong to take from individuals what they can accomplish by their own initiative and industry and give it to the community, so also it is an injustice and at the same time a grave evil and disturbance of right order to assign to a greater and higher association what lesser and subordinate organizations can do. For every social activity ought of its very nature to furnish help to the members of the body social, and never destroy and absorb them.*

SUBSIDIARITY IN OTHER DOCUMENTS OF CST:

Subsidiarity protects the intermediary groups of society. As Pope Francis points out, the well-being of these intermediate groups (especially the family) is essential to the good of society[10],

---

[10] Underlying the principle of the common good is respect for the human person as such, endowed with basic and inalienable rights ordered to his or her integral development. It has also to do with the overall welfare of society and the development of a variety of intermediate groups, applying the principle of subsidiarity. Outstanding among those groups is the family, as the basic cell of society. (Laudato Si', para. 157)

because local entities can provide benefits that global ones do not[11]. In fact, John Paul II notes that our human social needs are fulfilled not just in our interaction with the State, but most importantly through the other intermediary groups that make up society.[12]

For that reason, Popes John XXIII, Paul VI, and John Paul II lay out how subsidiarity should strengthen intermediary groups when it comes to property[13], individual well-being[14], and solving unemployment[15], respectively.

---

[11] At the same time, though, the local has to be eagerly embraced, for it possesses something that the global does not: it is capable of being a leaven, of bringing enrichment, of sparking mechanisms of subsidiarity. Universal fraternity and social friendship are thus two inseparable and equally vital poles in every society. To separate them would be to disfigure each and to create a dangerous polarization. (Fratelli tutti, para. 142)

[12] The social nature of man is not completely fulfilled in the State, but is realized in various intermediary groups, beginning with the family and including economic, social, political and cultural groups which stem from human nature itself and have their own autonomy, always with a view to the common good. (Centesimus Annus, para. 13)

[13] State and public ownership of property is very much on the increase today. This is explained by the exigencies of the common good, which demand that public authority broaden its sphere of activity. But here, too, the "principle of subsidiary function" must be observed. The State and other agencies of public law must not extend their ownership beyond what is clearly required by considerations of the common good properly understood, and even then there must be safeguards. Otherwise private ownership could be reduced beyond measure, or, even worse, completely destroyed. (Mater et Magistra, para. 117)

[14] It [political power] always intervenes with care for justice and with devotion to the common good, for which it holds final responsibility. It does not, for all that, deprive individuals and intermediary bodies of the field of activity and responsibility which are proper to them and which lead them to collaborate in the attainment of this common good. In fact, the true aim of all social activity should be to help individual members of the social body, but never to destroy or absorb them. (Octogesima Adveniens, para. 46)

[15] In the final analysis this overall concern [of unemployment] weighs on the shoulders of the State, but it cannot mean onesided centralization by the public authorities. Instead, what is in question is a just and rational *coordination,* within the framework of which the *initiative* of individuals, free groups and local work centres and complexes must be *safeguarded. (*Laborem Exercens, para. 18*)*

The most celebrated intermediary body in all Catholic social teaching is the family. It emphasizes that the State should allow the largest autonomy possible on how families govern themselves. In fact, Leo XIII states that only time the State can intervene in family affairs is when family members violate each other's mutual rights, or if the family has no other recourse for help in time of need[16].

Finally, Pope John XXIII invokes the concept of subsidiarity regarding international authorities who arbitrate justice between nations: such authority should not usurp what an individual nation and its own intermediary bodies are capable of accomplishing[17].

---

[16] True, if a family finds itself in exceeding distress, utterly deprived of the counsel of friends, and without any prospect of extricating itself, it is right that extreme necessity be met by public aid, since each family is a part of the commonwealth. In like manner, if within the precincts of the household there occur grave disturbance of mutual rights, public authority should intervene to force each party to yield to the other its proper due; for this is not to deprive citizens of their rights, but justly and properly to safeguard and strengthen them. But the rulers of the commonwealth must go no further; here, nature bids them stop. Paternal authority can be neither abolished nor absorbed by the State; for it has the same source as human life itself. (Rerum Novarum, para. 14)

[17] But it is no part of the duty of universal authority to limit the sphere of action of the public authority of individual States, or to arrogate any of their functions to itself. On the contrary, its essential purpose is to create world conditions in which the public authorities of each nation, its citizens and intermediate groups, can carry out their tasks, fulfill their duties and claim their rights with greater security. (Pacem in Terris, para. 141)

3) *Mater et Magistra,* <u>*Mother and Teacher*</u> (1961) On Christianity and Social Progress

The Historical Context

In the decades after *Quadragesimo Anno*, many Catholics put into practice Pius's call to reconstruct the social order. He regularly encouraged international "Catholic Action" groups (Catholic groups advocating social change) during his time as pope. These groups were active in Europe and the United States. In the U.S., Catholic Action groups effectively advocated for policies like decent housing and unemployment insurance for workers, both on a local and national level. By the 1960s, Catholic Action groups had died down because Catholics had increased options to get involved in political and economic life.

In 1961, Pope John XXIII wrote the encyclical *Mater et Magistra* to commemorate the seventieth anniversary of *Rerum Novarum*. Although Marxism and socialism were still influential in certain parts of the world, John XXIII wanted to focus on a different phenomenon affecting workers: the concept of "socialization"— the progressive multiplication of social relationships occurring throughout the world because of improvements in communication.

The Problem

Many of the unjust dynamics between factory workers and factory owners that occurred during the time of *Rerum Novarum* were now playing out in other sectors of the economy and in other countries as well.

III. NEW ASPECTS OF THE SOCIAL QUESTION

122. History shows with ever-increasing clarity that it is not only the relations between workers and managers that need to be re-established on the basis of justice and equity, but also those between the various branches of the economy, between areas of varying productivity within the same political community, and between countries with a different degree of social and economic development.

14

Because of these new realities, Pope John wanted to emphasize the following principle:

PRINCIPLE 3: THE COMMON GOOD

The *social conditions* where *everyone* (from poorest to richest) can maximize their human potential in *every aspect of life* (economic, emotional, spiritual).

Most economic/social behavior is based on balancing different self-interests: I advocate policies that benefit me, you advocate policies that benefit you, and we come to a mutual agreement. *Mater et Magistra* proposes something different. It expands on the concept of the "common good" mentioned in both *Rerum Novarum* and *Quadragesimo Anno*. Of course, the "common good" is not a new idea: it is present in the Old Testament of the Bible and even among ancient pagan philosophers. However, *Mater et Magistra* gives the initial working definition for Catholics in modern political times. This definition is expounded upon and repeated in the rest of Catholic social teaching. The job of the State, as well as all other social entities in society, is to keep this definition of the common good in mind when they make their decisions.

> *65. To this end, a sane view of the common good must be present and operative in men invested with public authority. They must take account of all those social conditions which favor the full development of human personality. Moreover, We consider it altogether vital that the numerous intermediary bodies and corporate enterprises—which are, so to say, the main vehicle of this social growth—be really autonomous, and loyally collaborate in pursuit of their own specific interests and those of the common good. For these groups must themselves necessarily present the form and substance of a true community, and this will only be the case if they treat their individual members as human persons and encourage them to take an active part in the ordering of their lives.*

THE COMMON GOOD IN CST

Pope Benedict reminds us that pursuing the common good requires every individual to consider every member of society[18].

In fact, multiple popes have stated that the government's job is not simply to avoid societal chaos, but also take active measures to promote the common good[19]. Governments must look at the diverse realities of its population and from there discern the common good[20], considering the human condition in all its aspects[21]. Different Popes have warned that States must not sacrifice the common good for the particular interests of the rich[22] and powerful[23], nor should they selectively apply rules to their

---

[18] Another important consideration is the common good. To love someone is to desire that person's good and to take effective steps to secure it. Besides the good of the individual, there is a good that is linked to living in society: the common good. It is the good of "all of us", made up of individuals, families and intermediate groups who together constitute society. It is a good that is sought not for its own sake, but for the people who belong to the social community and who can only really and effectively pursue their good within it. (Caritas in Veritate, para. 7)

[19] Government must not be thought a mere guardian of law and of good order, but rather must put forth every effort so that 'through the entire scheme of laws and institutions . . . both public and individual well-being may develop spontaneously out of the very structure and administration of the State.' (Quadragesimo Anno, para. 25). Pope Pius XI praising Leo XIII's stance in Rerum Novarum.

[20] Indeed, the common good embraces the sum of those conditions of the social life whereby men, families and associations more adequately and readily may attain their own perfection. Yet the people who come together in the political community are many and diverse, and they have every right to prefer divergent solutions. If the political community is not to be torn apart while everyone follows his own opinion, there must be an authority to direct the energies of all citizens toward the common good, not in a mechanical or despotic fashion, but by acting above all as a moral force which appeals to each one's freedom and sense of responsibility. (Gaudium et Spes, para. 74)

[21] In this connection, We would draw the attention of Our own sons to the fact that the common good is something which affects the needs of the whole man, body and soul. That, then, is the sort of good which rulers of States must take suitable measure to ensure. They must respect the hierarchy of values, and aim at achieving the spiritual as well as the material prosperity of their subjects. (Pacem in Terris, para. 57)

[22] The State cannot limit itself to "favoring one portion of the citizens", namely the rich and prosperous, nor can it "neglect the other", which clearly represents the majority of society. Otherwise, there would be a violation of that law of justice which ordains that every person should receive his due. (Centesimus Annus, para. 10)

[23] The failure of global summits on the environment make it plain that our politics are subject to technology and finance. There are too many

own advantage[24]. Rather, they should look to benefit every class in society[25].

---

special interests, and economic interests easily end up trumping the common good and manipulating information so that their own plans will not be affected. (Laudato Si', para. 54)

[24] Here there can be no room for disguising false intentions or placing the partisan interests of one country or group above the global common good. If rules are considered simply as means to be used whenever it proves advantageous, and to be ignored when it is not, uncontrollable forces are unleashed that cause grave harm to societies, to the poor and vulnerable, to fraternal relations, to the environment and to cultural treasures, with irretrievable losses for the global community. (Fratelli tutti, para. 257)

[25] Hereby, then, it lies in the power of a ruler to benefit every class in the State, and amongst the rest to promote to the utmost the interests of the poor; and this in virtue of his office, and without being open to suspicion of undue interference - since it is the province of the commonwealth to serve the common good. (Rerum Novarum, para. 32)

17

4) *Pacem In Terris, <u>Peace on Earth</u>* (1963)
On Peace among Peoples Based on Truth, Justice, Charity, and Liberty

The Historical Context

In addition to changing economic realities, Pope John XXIII wanted to address the constant threat of war between powerful nations. For that reason, two years after his previous encyclical, he wrote another one about world peace.

The Problem

Because more nations are liberated and no longer under official colonization, countries must create different ways of interacting that do not include a "superiority/inferiority" dynamic.

> *42. Finally, we are confronted in this modern age with a form of society which is evolving on entirely new social and political lines. Since all peoples have either attained political independence or are on the way to attaining it, soon no nation will rule over another and none will be subject to an alien power.*

> *43. Thus all over the world men are either the citizens of an independent State, or are shortly to become so; nor is any nation nowadays content to submit to foreign domination. The longstanding inferiority complex of certain classes because of their economic and social status, sex, or position in the State, and the corresponding superiority complex of other classes, is rapidly becoming a thing of the past.*

As societal relations got more complicated, Pope John XXIII highlighted our next economic principle:

PRINCIPLE 4: RIGHTS AND RESPONSIBILITIES

Every right we claim carries the responsibility to ensure others can enjoy that same right.

By virtue of living in society, we can claim certain rights (things society owes us). On the other side, we need to fulfill certain responsibilities (what we owe society). Although there is no official list of rights and responsibilities, different documents of Catholic social teaching have applauded the United Nations "Declaration of Human Rights," written as a result of the atrocities of World War II.

Reciprocity of Rights and Duties Between Persons

30. Once this is admitted, it follows that in human society one man's natural right gives rise to a corresponding duty in other men; the duty, that is, of recognizing and respecting that right. Every basic human right draws its authoritative force from the natural law, which confers it and attaches to it its respective duty. Hence, to claim one's rights and ignore one's duties, or only half fulfill them, is like building a house with one hand and tearing it down with the other.

Mutual Collaboration

31. Since men are social by nature, they must live together and consult each other's interests. That men should recognize and perform their respective rights and duties is imperative to a well ordered society. But the result will be that each individual will make his whole-hearted contribution to the creation of a civic order in which rights and duties are ever more diligently and more effectively observed.

RIGHTS AND RESPONSIBILITIES IN OTHER DOCUMENTS OF CST

From the very beginning of Catholic social teaching, the popes have recognized that determining the mutual rights and duties among societal members is a difficult task and susceptible to manipulation[26]. For example, if we focus only on the rights we claim for ourselves and ignore the rights others can claim for themselves, our individual demands will eventually become limitless and unreasonable[27].

---

[26] It is no easy matter to define the relative rights and mutual duties of the rich and of the poor, of capital and of labor. And the danger lies in this, that crafty agitators are intent on making use of these differences of opinion to pervert men's judgments and to stir up the people to revolt. (Rerum Novarum, para. 2)

[27] Individual rights, when detached from a framework of duties which

For that reason, Catholic social teaching tries to maintain a balance between the rights an individual can claim from society and what responsibilities an individual owes the rest of society. Here are a few examples: If I claim a right to private ownership, I have the duty to make sure all classes can claim the same opportunity for private ownership[28]. If our generation of human beings can claim the right to use nature's resources to fulfil our needs, then we have the responsibility to the next generation to make sure they can use nature's resources as well[29]. If a citizenry obligates its capable members to work, then the same citizenry has the responsibility to provide work opportunities[30].

Pope Paul VI, when reflecting on how human dignity and freedom play out in society, stresses the importance of educating the citizenry about their rights and corresponding responsibilities[31].

---

grants them their full meaning, can run wild, leading to an escalation of demands which is effectively unlimited and indiscriminate. An overemphasis on rights leads to a disregard for duties. (Caritas in Veritate, para. 43)

[28] The dignity of the human person "normally demands the right to the use of the goods of the earth, to which corresponds the fundamental obligation of granting an opportunity to possess property to all if possible." This demand arises from the moral dignity of work. It also guarantees "the conservation and perfection of a social order which makes possible a secure, even if modest, property to all classes of people." (Mater et Magistra, para. 114)

[29] "Tilling" refers to cultivating, ploughing or working, while "keeping" means caring, protecting, overseeing and preserving. This implies a relationship of mutual responsibility between human beings and nature. Each community can take from the bounty of the earth whatever it needs for subsistence, but it also has the duty to protect the earth and to ensure its fruitfulness for coming generations. (Laudato Si', para. 67)

[30] The obligation to earn one's bread by the sweat of one's brow also presumes the right to do so. A society in which this right is systematically denied, in which economic policies do not allow workers to reach satisfactory levels of employment, cannot be justified from an ethical point of view, nor can that society attain social peace. (Centesimus Annus, para. 43)

[31] This indicates the importance of education for life in society, in which there are called to mind, not only information on each one's rights, but also their necessary correlative: the recognition of the duties of each one in regard to others. The sense and practice of duty are themselves conditioned by self-mastery and by the acceptance of responsibility and of the limits placed upon the freedom of the individual or of the group.

In fact, Vatican II states that accepting the inherent responsibilities of social life is what gives our individual freedom new strength[32].

(Octogesima Adveniens, para. 24)

[32] Freedom acquires new strength, by contrast, when a man consents to the unavoidable requirements of social life, takes on the manifold demands of human partnership, and commits himself to the service of the human community. (Gaudium et Spes, para. 31)

5) *Gaudium et Spes, Joy and Hope* (1965)
On the Church in the Modern World

The Historical Context

In 1963, Pope John XXIII called the Second Vatican Council (a council is a meeting where the bishops from all around the world meet with the pope to talk about topics affecting all the Church). In our 2000-year history, we've had twenty-one such councils (twenty-two including the Council of Jerusalem in the New Testament). The Second Vatican Council (also known as Vatican II) was convened to talk about how the Church is to interact in the modern world. *Gaudium et Spes* is one of the documents produced from this council and is recognized as a document of Catholic social teaching.

The Problem

In order for human beings to adjust well to modern society, we need to understand what it means to be human. Many of our psychological, political, and social ills are results of our spiritual disorientation. Despite all the advances in the economy and our material well-being, we need spiritual orientation to discover our purpose and direction in life.

> *4) Never has the human race enjoyed such an abundance of wealth, resources and economic power, and yet a huge proportion of the worlds citizens are still tormented by hunger and poverty, while countless numbers suffer from total illiteracy. Never before has man had so keen an understanding of freedom, yet at the same time new forms of social and psychological slavery make their appearance. Although the world of today has a very vivid awareness of its unity and of how one man depends on another in needful solidarity, it is most grievously torn into opposing camps by conflicting forces. For political, social, economic, racial and ideological disputes still continue bitterly, and with them the peril of a war which would reduce everything to ashes. True, there is a growing exchange of ideas, but the very words by which key concepts are expressed take on quite different meanings in diverse ideological systems. Finally, man painstakingly searches for a better world, without a corresponding spiritual advancement.*

Influenced by such a variety of complexities, many of our contemporaries are kept from accurately identifying permanent values and adjusting them properly to fresh discoveries. As a result, buffeted between hope and anxiety and pressing one another with questions about the present course of events, they are burdened down with uneasiness. This same course of events leads men to look for answers; indeed, it forces them to do so.

With this spiritual orientation, *Gaudium et Spes* introduces our next principle:

PRINCIPLE 5: THE UNIVERSAL DESTINATION OF GOODS

The Earth's resources are meant to serve the common good.

We believe God created the world in abundance, and that there are enough resources in the world for everyone to have their basic needs met and enjoy a decent material life.

69. Whatever the forms of property may be, as adapted to the legitimate institutions of peoples, according to diverse and changeable circumstances, attention must always be paid to this universal destination of earthly goods. In using them, therefore, man should regard the external things that he legitimately possesses not only as his own but also as common in the sense that they should be able to benefit not only him but also others.

UNIVERSAL DESTINATION OF GOODS IN OTHER DOCUMENTS OF CST

A constant challenge that Popes have had regarding the universal destination of good is protecting this principle from both sides of the political spectrum. On one hand from socialists, who wanted to do away with private property and make only collective use of the Earth's resources; on the other hand, from libertarians who felt the Earth's resources belonged to anyone strong enough to take them.

Against the socialists, Catholic social teaching affirms private property because nature only provides the "raw material"- human labor is what transforms it into a goods people can enjoy[33]. It is true, however, that this raw material is not the exclusive property of an individual or group[34]. Public authorities have freedom to determine when the use of private property conflicts with the common good[35].

Against the libertarians, the popes have reiterated that the use of private property is not the highest human value[36]: if its use harms the common good[37], it is the State's responsibility to intervene[38].

---

[33] God gave the earth to the whole human race for the sustenance of all its members, without excluding or favoring anyone. This is *the foundation of the universal destination of the earth's goods.* The earth, by reason of its fruitfulness and its capacity to satisfy human needs, is God's first gift for the sustenance of human life. But the earth does not yield its fruits without a particular human response to God's gift, that is to say, without work. It is through work that man, using his intelligence and exercising his freedom, succeeds in dominating the earth and making it a fitting home. In this way, he makes part of the earth his own, precisely the part which he has acquired through work; this is *the origin of individual property.* Obviously, he also has the responsibility not to hinder others from having their own part of God's gift; indeed, he must cooperate with others so that together all can dominate the earth. (Centesimus Annus, para. 31)

[34] The fact that God has given the earth for the use and enjoyment of the whole human race can in no way be a bar to the owning of private property. For God has granted the earth to mankind in general, not in the sense that all without distinction can deal with it as they like, but rather that no part of it was assigned to any one in particular, and that the limits of private possession have been left to be fixed by man's own industry, and by the laws of individual races. (Rerum Novarum, para. 8)

[35] Therefore, public authority, under the guiding light always of the natural and divine law, can determine more accurately upon consideration of the true requirements of the common good, what is permitted and what is not permitted to owners in the use of their property. Moreover, Leo XIII wisely taught "that God has left the limits of private possessions to be fixed by the industry of men and institutions of peoples". (Quadragesimo Anno, para. 49)

[36] The principle of the subordination of private property to the universal destination of goods, and thus the right of everyone to their use, is a golden rule of social conduct and "the first principle of the whole ethical and social order". The Christian tradition has never recognized the right to private property as absolute or inviolable, and has stressed the social purpose of all forms of private property. (Laudato Si', para, 93)

[37] The right of private property may never be exercised to the detriment of the common good. When "private gain and basic community needs conflict with one another," it is for the public authorities "to seek a

The principal of the universal destination of goods praises the social function of material goods[39], a social function which Pope John Paul II famously called the "social mortgage"[40].

---

solution to these questions, with the active involvement of individual citizens and social groups." (Populorum Progressio, para, 23)

[38] Private ownership of property, including that of productive goods, is a natural right which the State cannot suppress. But it naturally entails a social obligation as well. It is a right which must be exercised not only for one's own personal benefit but also for the benefit of others. As for the State, its whole raison d'etre [reason for existing] is the realization of the common good in the temporal order. It cannot, therefore, hold aloof from economic matters. (Mater et Magistra, para. 19-20)

[39] All this brings out the positive meaning of the right to property: I care for and cultivate something that I possess, in such a way that it can contribute to the good of all. (Fratelli tutti, para. 143)

[40] It is necessary to state once more the characteristic principle of Christian social doctrine: the goods of this world are originally meant for all. The right to private property is valid and necessary, but it does not nullify the value of this principle. Private property, in fact, is under a "social mortgage," which means that it has an intrinsically social function, based upon and justified precisely by the principle of the universal destination of goods. (Sollicitudo Rei Socialis, para. 42)

6) *Populorum Progressio, <u>Progress of Peoples</u>* (1967) On the Development of Peoples

The Historical Context

John XXIII died during Vatican II, so Paul VI was the one who closed out the council. Shortly after, he wanted to expand on the international nature of social justice as articulated in the previous two social doctrine documents (*Pacem in Terris* and *Gaudium et Spes*).

The Problem

People in economically poor countries want to reach their potential, but currently can't. In order for them to do so, the international community needs a clear idea of what "development" is: if development is limited to measures of economic growth, the current struggles will continue. Pope Paul VI calls for a "complete development"—one that rids all material suffering (disease, abject poverty, etc.) and also provides social and political structures that allow humans to flourish in every sense of the word. A country's growth is the direct result of how well each citizen achieves his/her personal growth.

I. MAN'S COMPLETE DEVELOPMENT

6. They [people today] are continually striving to exercise greater personal responsibility; to do more, learn more, and have more so that they might increase their personal worth. And yet, at the same time, a large number of them live amid conditions which frustrate these legitimate desires. Moreover, those nations which have recently gained independence find that political freedom is not enough. They must also acquire the social and economic structures and processes that accord with man's nature and activity, if their citizens are to achieve personal growth and if their country is to take its rightful place in the international community.

Pope Paul VI's emphasis on our "complete development" has made *Populorum Progressio* the second most celebrated document of Catholic social teaching, behind *Rerum Novarum*.

26

As mentioned in the introduction, *Populorum Progressio* is the only other encyclical that prompted future popes to write commemorative documents.

PRINCIPLE 6: INTEGRAL HUMAN DEVELOPMENT

The different aspects of the human person must work together in harmony in order for real human flourishing to take place.

Paul VI noted that limiting "development" to only the economic sphere will leave members of every society empty and frustrated.

Authentic Development

14. The development We speak of here cannot be restricted to economic growth alone. To be authentic, it must be well rounded; it must foster the development of each man and of the whole man. As an eminent specialist on this question has rightly said: "We cannot allow economics to be separated from human realities, nor development from the civilization in which it takes place. What counts for us is man—each individual man, each human group, and humanity as a whole."

INTEGRAL HUMAN DEVELOPMENT IN CST

As mentioned in the principle of the common good, the human person has different aspects: the spiritual, the economic, the social, etc. For believers, the most important aspect of human life is the spiritual, since that puts all the other aspects in proper perspective[41].

One of the unsung contributions of Catholic social teaching is its ability to articulate how exaggerating one aspect of human life stunts a truly integral human development. In fact, Paul VI will later say that isolating man to his measurable behaviors is to ignore the totality of his being[42]. The most common example of

---

[41] Rest (combined with religious observances) disposes man to forget for a while the business of his everyday life, to turn his thoughts to things heavenly, and to the worship which he so strictly owes to the eternal Godhead. (Rerum Novarum, para. 41)
[42] Methodological necessity and ideological presuppositions too often lead the human sciences to isolate, in the various situations, certain

27

this reality is that economic wealth fails to leave people feeling truly rich[43].

But the popes have called out other exaggerations as having a similar effect. A few more examples: Pope John Paul II points out that reducing a person to only her social relationships ignores her capacity for choice and freedom[44]. Vatican II points out that for all our advances in technology, we are still forced to confront the reality that our life on earth will eventually end[45]. Pope Francis recognizes that demographic growth is compatible with integral human development, but unsustainable consumption is not[46].

---

aspects of man, and yet to give these an explanation which claims to be complete or at least an interpretation which is meant to be all-embracing from a purely quantitative or phenomenological point of view. This scientific reduction betrays a dangerous presupposition. To give a privileged position in this way to such an aspect of analysis is to mutilate man and, under the pretext of a scientific procedure, to make it impossible to understand man in his totality. (Octogesima Adveniens, para. 38)

[43] For what will it profit men to become expert in more wisely using their wealth, even to gaining the whole world, if thereby they suffer the loss of their souls? What will it profit to teach them sound principles of economic life if in unbridled and sordid greed they let themselves be swept away by their passion for property, so that "hearing the commandments of the Lord they do all things contrary"? (Quadragesimo Anno, para. 131)

[44] Socialism likewise maintains that the good of the individual can be realized without reference to his free choice, to the unique and exclusive responsibility which he exercises in the face of good or evil. Man is thus reduced to a series of social relationships, and the concept of the person as the autonomous subject of moral decision disappears, the very subject whose decisions build the social order. From this mistaken conception of the person there arise both a distortion of law, which defines the sphere of the exercise of freedom, and an opposition to private property. (Centesimus Annus, para. 13)

[45] He [man] bears in himself an eternal seed which cannot be reduced to sheer matter. All the endeavors of technology, though useful in the extreme, cannot calm his anxiety; for prolongation of biological life is unable to satisfy that desire for higher life which is inescapably lodged in his breast. (Gaudium et Spes, para. 18)

[46] Yet "while it is true that an unequal distribution of the population and of available resources creates obstacles to development and a sustainable use of the environment, it must nonetheless be recognized that demographic growth is fully compatible with an integral and shared development". To blame population growth instead of extreme and

A great articulation of how to go about achieving integral human development came on the 40th anniversary of *Populorum Progressio*, when Pope Benedict XVI called for all areas of human knowledge to work together, infusing among themselves a spirit of charity in truth[47] (more on that point in principle 11).

---

[47] Faced with the phenomena that lie before us, charity in truth requires first of all that we know and understand, acknowledging and respecting the specific competence of every level of knowledge. Charity is not an added extra, like an appendix to work already concluded in each of the various disciplines: it engages them in dialogue from the very beginning. The demands of love do not contradict those of reason. Human knowledge is insufficient and the conclusions of science cannot indicate by themselves the path towards integral human development. There is always a need to push further ahead: this is what is required by charity in truth. (Caritas in Veritate, para. 30)

7) *Octogesima Adveniens, Arrival of 80 Years* (1971) On the Eightieth Anniversary of Rerum Novarum

The Historical Context

For the eightieth anniversary of *Rerum Novarum*, Paul VI wanted to apply the teachings of that great encyclical to the "post-industrial" world—one in which the service industry has surpassed the manufacturing industry, and the complex social relations described in *Mater et Magistra* have become even more complicated.

The Problem

Eighty years after *Rerum Novarum*, harmful political ideologies are still being promoted and gaining popularity. Because political policy has such an outsized effect on economic well-being, Paul VI encourages all Catholics to utilize social groupings (both political and non-political) to promote mutual rights, responsibilities and the common good.

> *25. Political activity—need one remark that we are dealing primarily with an activity, not an ideology?—should be the projection of a plan of society which is consistent in its concrete means and in its inspiration, and which springs from a complete conception of man's vocation and of its differing social expressions. It is not for the State or even for political parties, which would be closed unto themselves, to try to impose an ideology by means that would lead to a dictatorship over minds, the worst kind of all. It is for cultural and religious groupings, in the freedom of acceptance which they presume, to develop in the social body, disinterestedly and in their own ways, those ultimate convictions on the nature, origin and end of man and society.*

Paul VI recognizes that in his day the world is so vast and complex that everyone should apply Catholic social teaching to their own unique situation. At the same time, every Catholic, regardless of their social situation, must be convinced that the Gospel will advance society. With that in mind, we have principle number 7:

PRINCIPLE 7: PARTICIPATION

Every societal entity must participate in discerning the common good and then take action to bring it about.

> *4. In the face of such widely varying situations it is difficult for us to utter a unified message and to put forward a solution which has universal validity. Such is not our ambition, nor is it our mission. It is up to the Christian communities to analyze with objectivity the situation which is proper to their own country, to shed on it the light of the Gospel's unalterable words and to draw principles of reflection, norms of judgment and directives for action from the social teaching of the Church.*

PARTICIPATION IN OTHER DOCUMENTS OF CST

Even in his previous encyclical, Paul VI noted that a lack of participation in society was due not just to material wealth, but also the inability to exercise power and thus deprive people of acting of their own initiative[48]. The church has no preference for which model of government a group of people employ, but rather it focuses on WHY a certain model is valuable. For example, it looks favorably on national procedures that allow citizens to participate in public affairs[49], and looks suspiciously on models that allow small ruling groups to use the State's power for individual interests[50].

---

[48] Then there are the flagrant inequalities not merely in the enjoyment of possessions, but even more in the exercise of power. In certain regions a privileged minority enjoys the refinements of life, while the rest of the inhabitants, impoverished and disunited, "are deprived of almost all possibility of acting on their own initiative and responsibility, and often subsist in living and working conditions unworthy of the human person." (Populorum Progressio, para. 9)

[49] Hence, the will to play one's role in common endeavors should be everywhere encouraged. Praise is due to those national procedures which allow the largest possible number of citizens to participate in public affairs with genuine freedom. Account must be taken, to be sure, of the actual conditions of each people and the decisiveness required by public authority. If every citizen is to feel inclined to take part in the activities of the various groups which make up the social body, these must offer advantages which will attract members and dispose them to serve others. (Gaudium et Spes, para. 31)

The Catholic church encourages the laity (people who aren't priests or nuns) to participate in improving worldly affairs[51] to the degree that their particular community allows[52]. Whether we belong to poor or rich countries[53], everyone has a role to play in discerning the common good and bringing it about[54].

---

[50] The Church values the democratic system inasmuch as it ensures the participation of citizens in making political choices, guarantees to the governed the possibility both of electing and holding accountable those who govern them, and of replacing them through peaceful means when appropriate. Thus she cannot encourage the formation of narrow ruling groups which usurp the power of the State for individual interests or for ideological ends. (Centesimus Annus, para. 46)

[51] It is appropriate to emphasize the preeminent role that belongs to the laity, both men and women, as was reaffirmed in the recent Assembly of the Synod. It is their task to animate temporal realities with Christian commitment, by which they show that they are witnesses and agents of peace and justice. (Sollicitudo Rei Socialis, para. 47)

[52] A natural consequence of men's dignity is unquestionably their right to take an active part in government, though their degree of participation will necessarily depend on the stage of development reached by the political community of which they are members. (Pacem in Terris, para. 73)

[53] It is a source of profound satisfaction to Us to see the prominent part which is being played by Catholic citizens of the less wealthy countries in the economic and social development of their own State. Then, too, the Catholics of the wealthier States are doing all they can to increase the effectiveness of the social and economic work that is being done for the poorer nations. (Mater et Magistra, para. 182-3)

[54] This means that "everyone has a fundamental role to play in a single great creative project: to write a new page of history, a page full of hope, peace and reconciliation". There is an "architecture" of peace, to which different institutions of society contribute, each according to its own area of expertise, but there is also an "art" of peace that involves us all. (Fratelli tutti, para. 231)

8) *Laborem Exercens, Through Work* (1981) On Human Work

The Historical Context

For the ninetieth anniversary of *Rerum Novarum*, Pope John Paul II wanted an in-depth look at human work. If we understand the meaning of human labor, we can better move toward a just employer-employee relationship that *Rerum Novarum* originally advocated.

The Problem

John Paul II's analysis of work is based on the "objective" and "subjective" dimension of work. The objective dimension focuses on the final product/service given for the benefit of society. The subjective dimension focuses on the fact that a *human* produced this beneficial product/service. This subjective dimension is especially in accord with what God had planned for human work in the beginning (see Gen. 1:28). The main distortion John Paul II sees is that the current economy focuses on humans as simply a factor of production and not as *the* producer of societal goods.

> 7. *A onesidedly materialistic civilization, which gives prime importance to the objective dimension of work, while the subjective dimension-everything in direct or indirect relationship with the subject of work-remains on a secondary level. In all cases of this sort, in every social situation of this type, there is a confusion or even a reversal of the order laid down from the beginning by the words of the Book of Genesis: man is treated as an instrument of production whereas he-he alone, independently of the work he does-ought to be treated as the effective subject of work and its true maker and creator.*

Because John Paul II thought that correcting this distortion of work the key to just work relationships, he dedicated this encyclical to the following principle:

PRINCIPLE 8: DIGNITY OF HUMAN WORK

A person's work should contribute to the common good and make him/her a better person in the process.

Jesus's work as a laborer shows all of us that the difficulty of any work (industrial, domestic, intellectual) is a gateway for us to be better humans—the exact way God designed work. For that reason, John Paul II says that the subjective dimension of work is more important than the objective dimension—a person's job should make her a better person, regardless of what kind of product/service she creates.

> 6. As *a person, man is therefore the subject of work.* As a person he works, he performs various actions belonging to the work process; independently of their objective content, these actions must all serve to realize his humanity, to fulfil the calling to be a person that is his by reason of his very humanity

DIGNITY OF HUMAN WORK IN CST

Because work is part of every human's vocation[55] and consists of everyday activity[56], people of faith must be conscious that our actions are part of God's creative action[57]. This action benefits both ourselves and society. Our work should be a unique expression of the unique gifts that God gave us[58]. As such, each

---

[55] Work thus belongs to the vocation of every person; indeed, man expresses and fulfils himself by working. At the same time, work has a "social" dimension through its intimate relationship not only to the family, but also to the common good, since "it may truly be said that it is only by the labour of working-men that States grow rich". (Centesimus Annus, para. 6)

[56] That a man should develop and perfect himself through his daily work—which in most cases is of a temporal character—is perfectly in keeping with the plan of divine Providence...In conducting their human affairs to the best of their ability, they must recognize that they are doing a service to humanity, in intimate union with God through Christ, and to God's greater glory. (Mater et Magistra, para. 256)

[57] This mandate concerns the whole of everyday activity as well. For while providing the substance of life for themselves and their families, men and women are performing their activities in a way which appropriately benefits society. They can justly consider that by their labor they are unfolding the Creator's work, consulting the advantages of their brother men, and are contributing by their personal industry to the realization in history of the divine plan. (Gaudium et Spes, para. 34)

[58] Whoever has received from the divine bounty a large share of temporal blessings, whether they be external and material, or gifts of the mind, has received them for the purpose of using them for the perfecting

34

worker will naturally leave his/her own unique imprint on the job's final manifestation[59].

A truly developed society creates the conditions so that a person, regardless of her place of work (an office, restaurant, manufacturing plant), is a better person as a result of working there[60]. On the contrary, if the working conditions are too harsh for a worker, it damages both the worker and society. Pope Pius XI lamented poor working conditions when he observed that when dead material enters a factory, it leaves better than it was before. However, when a live human being enters...he leaves worse[61]!

---

of his own nature, and, at the same time, that he may employ them, as the steward of God's providence, for the benefit of others. (Rerum Novarum, para. 22)

[59] Bent over a material that resists his efforts, the worker leaves his imprint on it, at the same time developing his own powers of persistence, inventiveness and concentration. Further, when work is done in common—when hope, hardship, ambition and joy are shared— it brings together and firmly unites the wills, minds and hearts of men. In its accomplishment, men find themselves to be brothers. (Populorum Progressio, para. 27)

[60] In a genuinely developed society, work is an essential dimension of social life, for it is not only a means of earning one's daily bread, but also of personal growth, the building of healthy relationships, self-expression and the exchange of gifts. Work gives us a sense of shared responsibility for the development of the world, and ultimately, for our life as a people. (Fratelli tutti, para. 162)

[61] And thus bodily labor, which Divine Providence decreed to be performed, even after original sin, for the good at once of man's body and soul, is being everywhere changed into an instrument of perversion; for dead matter comes forth from the factory ennobled, while men there are corrupted and degraded. (Quadragesimo Anno, para. 135)

9) *Sollicitudo Rei Socialis, Social Concern* (1987) The Twentieth Anniversary of *Populorum Progressio*

The Historical Context

John Paul II wrote this encyclical to commemorate the twentieth anniversary of *Populorum Progressio* and to reflect on the progress of nations in the current day. Of particular concern for John Paul II is that the world has been divided into different "blocks"—East versus West, and North versus South. By the "Eastern" block, he refers to communist countries, most notably the U.S.S.R. By the "Western" block, he refers to the vast majority of Western hemisphere countries that used some form of capitalism as their economic system. Even among capitalist countries, there's a growing divide between the wealthy "North" (Non-communist Europe and United States) and the poorer "South" (South America, Africa, and non-communist Asian countries). What most concerns John Paul II is that these different blocks seem to be headed in different directions in terms of the "full development" described by *Populorum Progressio*.

The Problem

Paul VI's vision of integral human development throughout the world has remained largely unfulfilled. John Paul II attributes this to the fact we still limit concept of development to mostly the economic sphere. As a result, poorer nations have stagnated in their economic development, while the rich ones have seen remarkable growth. This "superdevelopment" has left richer nations spiritually impoverished.

> 28. A disconcerting conclusion about the most recent period should serve to enlighten us: side-by-side with the miseries of underdevelopment, themselves unacceptable, we find ourselves up against a form of superdevelopment, equally inadmissible. because like the former it is contrary to what is good and to true happiness. This super-development, which consists in an excessive availability of every kind of material goods for the benefit of certain social groups, easily makes people slaves of "possession" and of immediate gratification,

with no other horizon than the multiplication or continual replacement of the things already owned with others still better. This is the so-called civilization of "consumption" or "consumerism," which involves so much "throwing-away" and "waste." An object already owned but now superseded by something better is discarded, with no thought of its possible lasting value in itself, nor of some other human being who is poorer.

Since *Mater et Magistra*, Catholic social teaching has defined the common good as the conditions under which every member of society can fully realize themselves, in every sense of the word. John Paul II introduces a term that means the opposite of the common good: "structures of sin."

PRINCIPLE 9: STRUCTURE OF SIN

Decisions (especially by those in civil authority) that actively create conditions opposed to the common good.

The pope identifies two motives for creating structures of sin: (1) the thirst for power (i.e., imposing my will onto others) and (2) the desire for profit at any price.

37. This general analysis, which is religious in nature, can be supplemented by a number of particular considerations to demonstrate that among the actions and attitudes opposed to the will of God, the good of neighbor and the "structures" created by them, two are very typical: on the one hand, the all-consuming desire for profit, and on the other, the thirst for power, with the intention of imposing one's will upon others. In order to characterize better each of these attitudes, one can add the expression: "at any price." In other words, we are faced with the absolutizing of human attitudes with all its possible consequences. Since these attitudes can exist independently of each other, they can be separated; however in today's world both are indissolubly united, with one or the other predominating.

STRUCTURES OF SIN IN CST

Some of the earliest documents condemn the rich's attempt to manipulate public policy in their own favor and at the expense of the common good. In fact, multiple popes have criticized public authority for becoming the "tool"[62] and "slave"[63] of the wealthy. Later on, Pope Paul VI will attribute these abuses of wealth and power as a significant cause for the "inhumane conditions" throughout the world[64].

Although we would intuitively associate structures of sin with unjust laws, structures of sin actually has more to do with the attitudes of people in decision making capacities. Pope Benedict notes the bad consequences of short-sighted economic attitudes[65], while Pope Paul VI laments the lack of concern for marginalized populations, which is why discrimination continues to occur[66]. Pope Francis condemns larger states trying to isolate the smaller ones and force them into dependency[67].

---

[62] Economic domination has taken the place of the open market. Unbridled ambition for domination has succeeded the desire for gain; the whole economic regime has become hard, cruel and relentless in frightful measure. As a consequence, even the public authority was becoming the tool of plutocracy, which was thus gaining a stranglehold on the entire world. (Mater et Magistra, para. 36)

[63] To these are to be added the grave evils that have resulted from an intermingling and shameful confusion of the functions and duties of public authority with those of the economic sphere - such as, one of the worst, the virtual degradation of the majesty of the State, which although it ought to sit on high like a queen and supreme arbitress, free from all partiality and intent upon the one common good and justice, is become a slave, surrendered and delivered to the passions and greed of men. (Quadragesimo Anno, para. 109)

[64] What are less than human conditions? The material poverty of those who lack the bare necessities of life, and the moral poverty of those who are crushed under the weight of their own self-love; oppressive political structures resulting from the abuse of ownership or the improper exercise of power, from the exploitation of the worker or unjust transactions. (Populorum Progressio, para. 21)

[65] Moreover, the human consequences of current tendencies towards a short-term economy — sometimes very short-term — need to be carefully evaluated. This requires *further and deeper reflection on the meaning of the economy and its goals*, as well as a profound and far-sighted revision of the current model of development, so as to correct its dysfunctions and deviations. (Caritas in Veritate, para. 32)

[66] Nevertheless various forms of discrimination continually reappear - ethnic cultural, religious, political and so on. In fact, human rights are still too often disregarded, if not scoffed at, or else they receive only formal recognition. In many cases legislation does not keep up with real situations. (Octogesima Adveniens, para. 23)

[67] There are powerful countries and large businesses that profit from this isolation and prefer to negotiate with each country separately. On

Finally, structures of sin also include necessary items lacking in society: Pope Francis points out that a lack of clear legal boundaries makes it easier for particular interests to hijack the common good and damage future generations[68]. Pope John Paul II notes that when society does not offer poor people a path to escape poverty, we can consider that a "structure of sin"[69].

---

the other hand, small or poor countries can sign agreements with their regional neighbors that will allow them to negotiate as a bloc and thus avoid being cut off, isolated and dependent on the great powers. Today, no state can ensure the common good of its population if it remains isolated. (Fratelli tutti, para. 153)

[68] We lack leadership capable of striking out on new paths and meeting the needs of the present with concern for all and without prejudice towards coming generations. The establishment of a legal framework which can set clear boundaries and ensure the protection of ecosystems has become indispensable; otherwise, the new power structures based on the techno-economic paradigm may overwhelm not only our politics but also freedom and justice. (Laudato Si', para. 53)

[69] In fact, for the poor, to the lack of material goods has been added a lack of knowledge and training which prevents them from escaping their state of humiliating subjection. Unfortunately, the great majority of people in the Third World still live in such conditions. (Centesimus Annus, para. 33)

10) Centesimus Annus, <u>100 Years</u> (1991) The Hundredth Anniversary of *Rerum Novarum*

The Historical Context

Four years after writing *Sollicitudo Rei Socialis*, Pope John Paul II wrote *Centesimus Annus* to commemorate the 100th anniversary of *Rerum Novarum*. During this time, much of the world was celebrating the end of various communist and socialist regimes.

The Problem

Even after 100 years, workers are being treated as secondary importance to the desire to make a profit. These warped priorities leave workers feeling alienated—the work they produce does not make them a better person. Furthermore, this alienation negatively affects the relationship between employer, employee, and consumer, damaging all of society.

> *41. Nevertheless alienation—and the loss of the authentic meaning of life—is a reality in Western societies too... Alienation is found also in work, when it is organized so as to ensure maximum returns and profits with no concern whether the worker, through his own labor, grows or diminishes as a person.... The concept of alienation needs to be led back to the Christian vision of reality, by recognizing in alienation a reversal of means and ends. When man does not recognize in himself and in others the value and grandeur of the human person, he effectively deprives himself of the possibility of benefitting from his humanity and of entering into that relationship of solidarity and communion with others for which God created him.*

PRINCIPLE 10: HUMAN DIGNITY

Every human being has an inherent value that all economic policies must respect.

After the fall of prominent communist countries in 1989, John Paul II recognized that many viewed capitalism as the "winner" as to which economic system can best serve humanity. However, he also reminds us that all economic systems must be subjected to higher moral principles. If capitalism is to be proposed as a model economic system for the world to follow, its good qualities (i.e., the free choice to produce and consume) should be balanced by the recognition that human beings are at the core ethical and religious beings, which means we should exercise our freedom in the larger context of what it means to be human.

42. Returning now to the initial question: can it perhaps be said that, after the failure of Communism, capitalism is the victorious social system, and that capitalism should be the goal of the countries now making efforts to rebuild their economy and society? Is this the model which ought to be proposed to the countries of the Third World which are searching for the path to true economic and civil progress?

The answer is obviously complex. If by "capitalism" is meant an economic system which recognizes the fundamental and positive role of business, the market, private property and the resulting responsibility for the means of production, as well as free human creativity in the economic sector, then the answer is certainly in the affirmative, even though it would perhaps be more appropriate to speak of a "business economy", "market economy" or simply "free economy". But if by "capitalism" is meant a system in which freedom in the economic sector is not circumscribed within a strong juridical framework which places it at the service of human freedom in its totality, and which sees it as a particular aspect of that freedom, the core of which is ethical and religious, then the reply is certainly negative.

HUMAN DIGNITY IN CST

A person's individual dignity is the basis for societal living,[70] and the job of all human institutions is to make sure our inherent value is protected and nurtured[71]. Whenever we attempt to solve

---

[70] Man as such, far from being an object or, as it were, an inert element in society, is rather its subject, its basis and its purpose; and so must he be esteemed. (Pacem in Terris, para. 26)

[71] Therefore, although rightful differences exist between men, the equal dignity of persons demands that a more humane and just condition of

41

a societal problem, the proposal must take into account the totality of man, especially his dignity[72]. All the effects of our economic decisions, including work relations[73], must respect the dignity of all people involved[74]. Human beings must be treated differently than material objects and every human being deserves the same respect regardless of external circumstances she finds herself in[75]. In fact, people from across generations and classes had come together to protest for social solutions that respect everyone's inherent value[76].

---

life be brought about...Human institutions, both private and public, must labor to minister to the dignity and purpose of man. (Gaudium et Spes, para. 29)

[72] We must nevertheless state most emphatically that no statement of the problem and no solution to it is acceptable which does violence to man's essential dignity; those who propose such solutions base them on an utterly materialistic conception of man himself and his life. (Mater et Magistra, para. 191)

[73] The Church considers it her task always to call attention to the dignity and rights of those who work, to condemn situations in which that dignity and those rights are violated, and to help to guide the above-mentioned changes so as to ensure authentic progress by man and society. (Laborem Exercens, para. 1)

[74] Human beings too are creatures of this world, enjoying a right to life and happiness, and endowed with unique dignity. So we cannot fail to consider the effects on people's lives of environmental deterioration, current models of development and the throwaway culture. (Laudato Si', para. 43)

[75] The dignity of others is to be respected in all circumstances, not because that dignity is something we have invented or imagined, but because human beings possess an intrinsic worth superior to that of material objects and contingent situations. This requires that they be treated differently. That every human being possesses an inalienable dignity is a truth that corresponds to human nature apart from all cultural change. (Fratelli tutti, para. 231)

[76] The Church affirmed clearly and forcefully that every individual — whatever his or her personal convictions — bears the image of God and therefore deserves respect. Often, the vast majority of people identified themselves with this kind of affirmation, and this led to a search for forms of protest and for political solutions more respectful of the dignity of the person. (Centesimus Annus, para. 22)

11) Caritas in Veritate, _Charity in Truth_ (2009) Integral Human Development in Charity and Truth

The Historical Context

Pope Benedict XVI wrote this encyclical to celebrate the fortieth anniversary of _Populorum Progressio_. This encyclical was delayed two years because of the financial crisis of 2007–2008.

The Problem

Forty years after _Populorum Progressio_, the integral development of peoples still isn't going well. In Benedict's estimation, our economic system cannot only survive off justice (the attitude of "what's mine is mine, what's yours is yours"). The human family needs to infuse the Christian concept of charity (what's mine is yours) into our economic transactions. In societal living, simple justice would mean we all complete our duties and exercise our rights. Charity, on the other hand, would mean our conscious integration of mercy and graciousness to our societal relationships. This attitude of "charity-infused justice" is the most effective way of realizing the common good.

> _6. Charity goes beyond justice, because to love is to give, to offer what is "mine" to the other; but it never lacks justice, which prompts us to give the other what is "his", what is due to him by reason of his being or his acting. I cannot "give" what is mine to the other, without first giving him what pertains to him in justice. If we love others with charity, then first of all we are just towards them...charity transcends justice and completes it in the logic of giving and forgiving. The earthly city is promoted not merely by relationships of rights and duties, but to an even greater and more fundamental extent by relationships of gratuitousness, mercy and communion. Charity always manifests God's love in human relationships as well, it gives theological and salvific value to all commitment for justice in the world._

When reflecting on which societal system would benefit humanity, both Benedict and John Paul II like to think of a system containing three subjects: the State (governmental entities), the market (business entities), and civil society (the majority of societal entities that don't fall under "business" or "government": family, church, social clubs, etc.)[77]. Infusing Christian charity into these three subjects brings us to principle 11:

PRINCIPLE 11: THE LOGIC OF THE GIFT

Every aspect of society needs to allow for gratuitousness- the ability for a person to give without expecting anything in return.

Benedict points out that each human activity has its own "logic"—characteristics that allow it to function. Different parts of society are usually dominated by a particular logic:
-The State operates largely on the logic of "duty" – I enjoy certain rights in society, and therefore have the responsibility to make sure others can enjoy the same rights I enjoy.
 -The market operates largely on the logic of "exchange"- I give you something (usually money), you provide me with some sort of product or service.
-The civil society is, as Benedict and John Paul II say, is the most natural setting for the "logic of the gift": I give to you, and I don't expect anything in return.
The only way for economic policy (i.e., the intersection of the market and the State) to reach its full potential is to allow for the logic of the gift (gratuitousness) to be present. If the State and market only stay with respective area of influence, both sectors will stagnate:

> *35. In fact, if the market is governed solely by the principle of the equivalence in value of exchanged goods, it cannot produce the social cohesion that it requires in order to function well. Without internal forms of solidarity and mutual trust, the market cannot completely fulfil its proper economic function.*

---

[77] My predecessor John Paul II drew attention to this question in *Centesimus Annus,* when he spoke of the need for a system with three subjects: the *market*, the *State* and *civil society*. He saw civil society as the most natural setting for an *economy of gratuitousness* and fraternity, but did not mean to deny it a place in the other two settings. (Caritas in Veritate, para. 38)

39. When both the logic of the market and the logic of the State come to an agreement that each will continue to exercise a monopoly over its respective area of influence, in the long term much is lost: solidarity in relations between citizens, participation and adherence, actions of gratuitousness, all of which stand in contrast with giving in order to acquire (the logic of exchange) and giving through duty (the logic of public obligation, imposed by State law).

THE LOGIC OF THE GIFT IN CST

When we practice gratuitousness, we are participating in God's very essence as a communion of love and thus realizing our full potential as human beings[78]. The key is to freely give of ourselves to other people, not simply ideals or theories[79]. Appling the logic of the gift means going beyond the logic of duty (i.e., respecting others' rights): by definition it can't be enforced by human law[80], because it includes forgiveness and reconciliation[81].

---

[78] He [Jesus] implied a certain likeness between the union of the divine Persons, and the unity of God's sons in truth and charity. This likeness reveals that man, who is the only creature on earth which God willed for itself, cannot fully find himself except through a sincere gift of himself. (Gaudium et Spes, para. 24)

[79] Indeed, it is through the free gift of self that man truly finds himself. This gift is made possible by the human person's essential "capacity for transcendence". Man cannot give himself to a purely human plan for reality, to an abstract ideal or to a false utopia. As a person, he can give himself to another person or to other persons, and ultimately to God, who is the author of his being and who alone can fully accept his gift. (Centesimus Annus, para. 41)

[80] "Of that which remains give alms" [quoting Luke 11:41]. It is a duty, not of justice (save in extreme cases), but of Christian charity - a duty not enforced by human law. But the laws and judgments of men must yield place to the laws and judgments of Christ the true God, who in many ways urges on His followers the practice of almsgiving – "It is more blessed to give than to receive" [quoting Acts 20:35]. (Rerum Novarum, para. 22)

[81] In the light of faith, solidarity seeks to go beyond itself, to take on the specifically Christian dimension of total gratuity, forgiveness and reconciliation. One's neighbor is then not only a human being with his or her own rights and a fundamental equality with everyone else, but becomes the living image of God the Father, redeemed by the blood of Jesus Christ and placed under the permanent action of the Holy Spirit. (Sollicitudo Rei Socialis, para. 40)

45

Popes have proposed specific examples of what the logic of gift would look like when applied to economic realities. Pope Francis applauds a country's effort to accept not only immigrants that can benefit the economy (like scientists or investors), but also the immigrants who can't offer any immediate economic value[82]. Pope Pius XI commends the use of extra wealth to create productive jobs for others as an act of "munificence" (graciousness)[83]. In our modern economic times, we need to apply logic of the gift to liberate people from dehumanizing social conditions[84].

---

[82] I do not wish to limit this presentation to a kind of utilitarian approach. There is always the factor of "gratuitousness": the ability to do some things simply because they are good in themselves, without concern for personal gain or recompense. Gratuitousness makes it possible for us to welcome the stranger, even though this brings us no immediate tangible benefit. Some countries, though, presume to accept only scientists or investors. (Fratelli tutti, para. 139)

[83] Expending larger incomes so that opportunity for gainful work may be abundant, provided, however, that this work is applied to producing really useful goods, ought to be considered, as We deduce from the principles of the Angelic Doctor, an outstanding exemplification of the virtue of munificence and one particularly suited to the needs of the times. (Quadragesimo Anno, para. 51)

[84] This liberation starts with the interior freedom that men must find again with regard to their goods and their powers; they will never reach it except through a transcendent love for man, and, in consequence, through a genuine readiness to serve. (Octogesima Adveniens, para. 45)

12) *Laudato Si', <u>Praise Be to You</u>* (2015) On Care for Our Common Home

The Historical Context

Pope Francis wanted to dedicate a social encyclical to how our economic activity affects the environment.

The Problem

We view nature as an object to be exploited and manipulated though technology, rather than a creature to live in harmony with. As a result of this mentality, our way of producing things cause bad effects on the environment.

> *II. THE GLOBALIZATION OF THE TECHNOCRATIC PARADIGM*
>
> *106. The basic problem goes even deeper: it is the way that humanity has taken up technology and its development according to an undifferentiated and one-dimensional paradigm...Men and women have constantly intervened in nature, but for a long time this meant being in tune with and respecting the possibilities offered by the things themselves. It was a matter of receiving what nature itself allowed, as if from its own hand. Now, by contrast, we are the ones to lay our hands on things, attempting to extract everything possible from them while frequently ignoring or forgetting the reality in front of us...It is based on the lie that there is an infinite supply of the earth's goods, and this leads to the planet being squeezed dry beyond every limit. It is the false notion that "an infinite quantity of energy and resources are available, that it is possible to renew them quickly, and that the negative effects of the exploitation of the natural order can be easily absorbed".*

With that problem in mind, we come to principle 12:

PRINCIPLE 12: CARE FOR THE ENVIRONMENT

All economic polices must consider its effect on the environment.

Pope Francis invites us to leave behind an "anthropocentric" mentality—a mentality that values the environment only to the extent that it is useful for human production and consumption. Rather, we must realize that the earth has value for its own sake. In our quest to produce more material goods and services, we must take into our account our impact on the environment.

> 69. By virtue of our unique dignity and our gift of intelligence, we are called to respect creation and its inherent laws, for "the Lord by wisdom founded the earth" (Prov 3:19). In our time, the Church does not simply state that other creatures are completely subordinated to the good of human beings, as if they have no worth in themselves and can be treated as we wish...Each creature possesses its own particular goodness and perfection...Each of the various creatures, willed in its own being, reflects in its own way a ray of God's infinite wisdom and goodness. Man must therefore respect the particular goodness of every creature, to avoid any disordered use of things.

CARE FOR THE ENVIRONMENT IN CST

Surprisingly, the earliest references in Catholic social teaching to the Earth's resources wasn't about its scarcity, but rather its abundance[85]. Early documents focused on land abundance because land ownership was the primary way to economic prosperity[86]. Later documents also encourage the proper use of land to help the poor lift themselves from poverty[87] as they utilize the various riches of nature[88].

---

[85] The fact that God has given the earth for the use and enjoyment of the whole human race can in no way be a bar to the owning of private property. For God has granted the earth to mankind in general, not in the sense that all without distinction can deal with it as they like, but rather that no part of it was assigned to any one in particular, and that the limits of private possession have been left to be fixed by man's own industry, and by the laws of individual races. (Rerum Novarum, para. 8)
[86] Hence, man not only should possess the fruits of the earth, but also the very soil, inasmuch as from the produce of the earth he has to lay by provision for the future. Man's needs do not die out, but forever recur; although satisfied today, they demand fresh supplies for tomorrow. Nature accordingly must have given to man a source that is stable and remaining always with him, from which he might look to draw continual supplies. (Rerum Novarum, para. 7)
[87] In view of the special difficulties of agriculture relative to the raising

By the mid-20th century, population growth caused worry about the earth's capacity to produce food, causing some nations to advocate population control measures. The Catholic Church affirmed that there are enough resources on the planet for the emerging population if we utilize the sciences to cultivate the earth's resources efficiently[89].

An important tone shift came in *Octogesima Adveniens*, when Pope Paul VI recognized that we were becoming so irresponsible in our use of the environment that we were endangering not only our fellow human beings, but also the Earth itself[90]. John Paul calls for us to take the Earth's natural

---

and selling of produce, country people must be helped both to increase and to market what they produce, and to introduce the necessary development and renewal and also obtain a fair income. Otherwise, as too often happens, they will remain in the condition of lower-class citizens. Let farmers themselves, especially young ones, apply themselves to perfecting their professional skill, for without it, there can be no agricultural advance. (Gaudium et Spes, para. 66)

[88] To be able through his work to make these resources bear fruit, man takes over ownership of small parts of the various riches of nature: those beneath the ground, those in the sea, on land, or in space. He takes all these things over by making them his workbench. He takes them over through work and for work. (Laborem Exercens, para. 12)

[89] Truth to tell, we do not seem to be faced with any immediate or imminent world problem arising from the disproportion between the increase of population and the supply of food. Arguments to this effect are based on such unreliable and controversial data that they can only be of very uncertain validity. Besides, the resources which God in His goodness and wisdom has implanted in Nature are well-nigh inexhaustible, and He has at the same time given man the intelligence to discover ways and means of exploiting these resources for his own advantage and his own livelihood. Hence, the real solution of the problem is not to be found in expedients which offend against the divinely established moral order and which attack human life at its very source, but in a renewed scientific and technical effort on man's part to deepen and extend his dominion over Nature. The progress of science and technology that has already been achieved opens up almost limitless horizons in this held. (Mater et Magistra, para. 188-189)

[90] Man is suddenly becoming aware that by an ill-considered exploitation of nature he risks destroying it and becoming in his turn the victim of this degradation. Not only is the material environment becoming a permanent menace - pollution and refuse, new illness and absolute destructive capacity - but the human framework is no longer under man's control, thus creating an environment for tomorrow which

cycles into account when economic planning, using the phrase "ecological concern"[91]. Pope Benedict XVI reminds us to strike a balance: on one hand, recognizing humans' special place in nature[92]; on the other hand, respecting nature's internal workings rather than exploiting them[93].

---

may well be intolerable. This is a wide-ranging social problem which concerns the entire human family. (Octogesima Adveniens, para. 21)

[91] Among today's positive signs we must also mention a greater realization of the limits of available resources, and of the need to respect the integrity and the cycles of nature and to take them into account when planning for development, rather than sacrificing them to certain demagogic ideas about the latter. Today this is called ecological concern. (Sollicitudo Rei Socialis, para. 26)

[92] It should also be stressed that it is contrary to authentic development to view nature as something more important than the human person. This position leads to attitudes of neo-paganism or a new pantheism — human salvation cannot come from nature alone, understood in a purely naturalistic sense. (Caritas in Veritate, para. 48)

[93] It is also necessary to reject the opposite position, which aims at total technical dominion over nature, because the natural environment is more than raw material to be manipulated at our pleasure; it is a wondrous work of the Creator containing a "grammar" which sets forth ends and criteria for its wise use, not its reckless exploitation. (Caritas in Veritate, para. 48)

13) *Fratelli tutti, <u>All Brothers</u>* (2020) On Fraternity and Social Friendship

The Historical Context

The previous decades of economic trends in financial markets, global trade, and nationalist pride have led to a lot of "haves" and "have nots" in the world. This prompted Pope Francis to begin writing an encyclical on social friendship that transcends both national boundaries and economic class.

The Problem

Many of the habits we've created (both economic and social) have caused a more fragmented society. This reality was exaggerated by the Covid health pandemic of 2020 and confirmed that we need to make fundamental changes, not simply do a more efficient version of what we've been currently doing.

> *7. As I was writing this letter, the Covid-19 pandemic unexpectedly erupted, exposing our false securities. Aside from the different ways that various countries responded to the crisis, their inability to work together became quite evident. For all our hyper-connectivity, we witnessed a fragmentation that made it more difficult to resolve problems that affect us all. Anyone who thinks that the only lesson to be learned was the need to improve what we were already doing, or to refine existing systems and regulations, is denying reality.*

To develop the "social friendship" that Pope Francis, calls for, we need to develop principle 13:

PRINCIPLE 13: SOLIDARITY

All societal entities (from individuals to nations) must take responsibility for each other's well-being.

The fact that we are all human connects us in a way that makes us morally responsible for each other. Catholic social teaching calls this notion "solidarity." Pope Francis points out that solidarity is not simply sporadic actions, but rather fundamental attitude changes.

> *116. Solidarity is a word that is not always well received; in certain situations, it has become a dirty word, a word that dare not be said. Solidarity means much more than engaging in sporadic acts of generosity. It means thinking and acting in terms of community. It means that the lives of all are prior to the appropriation of goods by a few. It also means combatting the structural causes of poverty, inequality, the lack of work, land and housing, the denial of social and labour rights.*

SOLIDARITY IN CST

Like the common good, solidarity is a phrase that has existed throughout human history. In fact, other documents of Catholic social teaching have made solidarity a pillar of its content. For example Populorum Progressio was praised for its international outlook[94] and emphasis on solidarity in the development of nations[95]. Like Pope Francis, John Paul II also tried to rescue the phrase "solidarity" from a shallow understanding, contrasting the superficial sympathy associated with the word to the commitment and responsibility that solidarity actually requires[96]. He holds the 19th century industrial workers coming together

---

[94] The second point of originality of Populorum Progressio is shown by the breadth of outlook open to what is commonly called the "social question." In fact, the Encyclical *Mater et Magistra* of Pope John XXIII had already entered into this wider outlook, and the Council had echoed the same in the Constitution Gaudium et Spes. However, the social teaching of the Church had not yet reached the point of affirming with such clarity that the social question has acquired a worldwide dimension. (Sollicitudo Rei Socialis, para. 9)

[95] Each man is also a member of society; hence he belongs to the community of man. It is not just certain individuals but all men who are called to further the development of human society as a whole...The reality of human solidarity brings us not only benefits but also obligations. (Populorum Progressio, para. 17)

[96] This then is not a feeling of vague compassion or shallow distress at the misfortunes of so many people, both near and far. On the contrary, it is a firm and persevering determination to commit oneself to the common good; that is to say to the good of all and of each individual, because we are all really responsible for all." (Sollicitudo Rei Socialis, para. 38)

from their different spheres to protest their de-humanizing working conditions as an example of true solidarity[97]. In the same vein, Pope Francis calls on this generation take responsibility for the well-being of future ones, utilizing the term "intergenerational solidarity[98]".

Solidarity is focused not only on ending injustice[99], but also in uniting humanity in a way that mere legislation would never be able to do[100]. In fact, Catholics do not view the richer classes as

---

[97] This question and the problems connected with it gave rise to a just social reaction and caused the impetuous emergence of a great burst of solidarity between workers, first and foremost industrial workers. The call to solidarity and common action addressed to the workers-especially to those engaged in narrowly specialized, monotonous and depersonalized work in industrial plants, when the machine tends to dominate man - was important and eloquent from the point of view of social ethics. It was the reaction *against the degradation of man as the subject of work,* and against the unheard-of accompanying exploitation in the field of wages, working conditions and social security for the worker. This reaction united the working world in a community marked by great solidarity. (Laborem Exercens, para. 8)

[98] The global economic crises have made painfully obvious the detrimental effects of disregarding our common destiny, which cannot exclude those who come after us. We can no longer speak of sustainable development apart from intergenerational solidarity. Once we start to think about the kind of world we are leaving to future generations, we look at things differently… Intergenerational solidarity is not optional, but rather a basic question of justice, since the world we have received also belongs to those who will follow us. (Laudato Si', para. 159)

[99] For justice alone can, if faithfully observed, remove the causes of social conflict but can never bring about union of minds and hearts. Indeed all the institutions for the establishment of peace and the promotion of mutual help among men, however perfect these may seem, have the principal foundation of their stability in the mutual bond of minds and hearts whereby the members are united with one another. If this bond is lacking, the best of regulations come to naught, as we have learned by too frequent experience. And so, then only will true cooperation be possible for a single common good when the constituent parts of society deeply feel themselves members of one great family and children of the same Heavenly Father. (Quadragesimo Anno, para. 137)

[100] In many cases legislation does not keep up with real situations. Legislation is necessary, but it is not sufficient for setting up true relationships of justice and equity…If, beyond legal rules, there is really no deeper feeling of respect for and service to others, then even

53

the enemy of the poorer ones[101], but rather all classes must work together for the common good[102].

---

equality before the law can serve as an alibi for flagrant discrimination, continued exploitation and actual contempt. Without a renewed education in solidarity, an overemphasis of equality can give rise to an individualism in which each one claims his own rights without wishing to be answerable for the common good. (Octogesima Adveniens, para. 23)

[101] The great mistake made in regard to the matter now under consideration is to take up with the notion that class is naturally hostile to class, and that the wealthy and the working men are intended by nature to live in mutual conflict. So irrational and so false is this view that the direct contrary is the truth. (Rerum Novarum, 19)

[102] In using their various organizations, agricultural workers—as indeed all other classes of workers—must always be guided by moral principles and respect for the civil law. They must try to reconcile their rights and interests with those of other classes of workers, and even subordinate the one to the other if the common good demands it. (Mater et Magistra, para. 147)

CONCLUSION

As of this writing, *Fratelli tutti* is the most recent document in the Catholic social teaching tradition. From *Rerum Novarum* to *Fratelli tutti*, the Catholic Church has had many things to say about societal living in modern times. Popes have continually tried to apply the Gospel of Jesus Christ to specific societal situations so that all people can live in peace with one another. And as society continues to change, Catholic social teaching will be there to give guidance and direction to those changes.

STILL HUNGRY FOR MORE?

As you can see by the excerpts, the documents of Catholic social teaching are at times dense. Making the jump to reading hundreds of these types of paragraphs might leave you frustrated.

A good next step would be reading the Vatican document, "Vocation of a Business Leader: A Reflection." This 2013 document goes over themes mentioned in this book, especially the worker-employer relationship analyzed in *Rerum Novarum* and its sequels.

After that, I'd read two sections of the "Catechism of the Catholic Church" regarding social life: paragraphs 1877–1946 discuss the "human community" and paragraphs 2401–2463 discuss the seventh commandment ("thou shalt not steal").

After that, give the "Compendium of the Social Doctrine of the Church" a try.

And after the compendium, try the thirteen foundational documents.

I hope you enjoyed reading this book as much as I did writing it. I've always enjoyed learning about economics and economic policy. My first exposure to Catholic social teaching was at a parish talk, where we learned about different terms unique to this branch of our faith (terms like solidarity, the common good and subsidiarity). I grew to appreciate it even more when I learned that these teachings were formed out of real problems occurring in the world and that these moral guidelines had a real impact on people's lives. It made me confident that the concepts of Catholic social teaching could improve our world situation both now and in the future. Even now, when I read articles about economics or talk about politics with loved ones, I do so through the lens of these great moral principles.

Thanks again for reading, I hope this book has helped construct a firm foundation of how Catholics should approach modern economic policy!

APPENDIX 1: LINKS TO CATHOLIC SOCIAL TEACHING DOCUMENTS

Rerum Novarum
http://www.vatican.va/content/leo-xiii/en/encyclicals/documents/hf_l-xiii_enc_15051891_rerum-novarum.html

Quadragesimo Anno
http://www.vatican.va/content/pius-xi/en/encyclicals/documents/hf_p-xi_enc_19310515_quadragesimo-anno.html

Mater et Magistra
http://www.vatican.va/content/john-xxiii/en/encyclicals/documents/hf_j-xxiii_enc_15051961_mater.html

Pacem in Terris
http://www.vatican.va/content/john-xxiii/en/encyclicals/documents/hf_j-xxiii_enc_11041963_pacem.html

Gaudium et Spes
http://www.vatican.va/archive/hist_councils/ii_vatican_council/documents/vat-ii_const_19651207_gaudium-et-spes_en.html

Populorum Progressio
http://www.vatican.va/content/paul-vi/en/encyclicals/documents/hf_p-vi_enc_26031967_populorum.html

Octogesima Adveniens
http://www.vatican.va/content/paul-vi/en/apost_letters/documents/hf_p-vi_apl_19710514_octogesima-adveniens.html

Laborem Exercens
http://www.vatican.va/content/john-paul-ii/en/encyclicals/documents/hf_jp-ii_enc_14091981_laborem-exercens.html

Sollicitudo Rei Socialis
http://www.vatican.va/content/john-paul-ii/en/encyclicals/documents/hf_jp-ii_enc_30121987_sollicitudo-rei-socialis.html

Centesimus Annus
http://www.vatican.va/content/john-paul-ii/en/encyclicals/documents/hf_jp-ii_enc_01051991_centesimus-annus.html

Caritas in Veritate
http://www.vatican.va/content/benedict-xvi/en/encyclicals/documents/hf_ben-xvi_enc_20090629_caritas-in-veritate.html

Laudato Si'
http://www.vatican.va/content/francesco/en/encyclicals/documents/papa-francesco_20150524_enciclica-laudato-si.html

Fratelli tutti
https://www.vatican.va/content/francesco/en/encyclicals/documents/papa-francesco_20201003_enciclica-fratelli-tutti.html

APPENDIX 2: A QUICK REFERENCE OF THE 13 PRINCIPLES

Just Work Relations
Just economic relations are a necessary foundation for peace.

"It must be remembered that the market does not exist in a pure state. It is shaped by the cultural configuration which define it and give it direction" (Caritas in Veritate, 36)

Subsidiarity
State authority should not usurp what individuals and intermediary entities are capable of accomplishing.

"It does not, for all that, deprive individuals and intermediary bodies of the fields of activity and responsibility which are proper to them and which lead them to collaborate in the attainment of this common good." (Octogesima Adveniens, 46)

Common Good
The social conditions where everyone (from poorest to richest) can maximize their human potential in every aspect of life (economic, emotional, spiritual).

"Both public and individual well-being may develop spontaneously out the very structure and administration of the State" (Quadragesimo Anno, 25)

Rights and Responsibilities
Every right we claim carries the duty to ensure others can enjoy the same right.

"To claim one's rights and ignore one's duties, or only half fulfill them, is like building a house with one hand and tearing it down with the other." (Pacem in Terris, 30)

Universal Destination of Goods
God has put enough "raw material" in the Earth for all of us to cultivate and enjoy.

"God gave the earth to the whole human race for the sustenance of all its members, without excluding or favoring anyone" (Centesimus Annus, 31)

Integral Human Development

Human development cannot be limited to economic growth alone. It must involve each person in his/her wholeness.

"We cannot allow economics to be separated from human realities, nor development from the civilization in which it takes place" (Populorum Progressio, 14)

Participation
Citizens should utilize social groupings (both political and non-political) to promote mutual rights, responsibilities and the common good.

"It is up to the Christian communities to analyze with objectivity the situation which is proper to their own country, to shed on it the light of the Gospel's unalterable words and to draw principles of reflection, norms of judgement and directives for action from the social teaching of the Church." (Octogesima Adveniens, 4)

Dignity of Human Work
A person's job should make her a better person, regardless of what kind of product/service she creates.

"Work thus belongs to the vocation of every person; indeed, man expresses and fulfils himself by working. At the same time, work has a social dimension through its intimate relationship not only to the family, but also to the common good, since 'it may truly be said that it is only by the labor of working-men that States grow rich.'" (Centesimus Annus, 6)

Structures of Sin
Attitudes of decision makers that run against the common good.

"In fact, human rights are still too often disregarded, if not scoffed at, or else the receive only formal recognition. In many cases, legislation does not keep up with real situations." (Octogesima Adveniens, 23)

Human Dignity
We cannot offer economic policies that harm a person's dignity or reduce him to a material entity.

"Alienation is also found in work, when it is organized so as to ensure maximum returns and profits with no concern whether the worker, through his own labor, grows or diminishes as a person." (Centesimus Annus, 41)

The Logic of the Gift
Charity must be able to manifest itself every area of society, not only in the non-profit sphere.

"When both the logic of the market and the logic of the State come to an agreement that each will continue to exercise a monopoly over its respective area of influence, in the long term much is lost." (Caritas in Veritate, 39)

Care for the Environment
Our economic policy must strive to live in harmony with nature rather than exploit it through technology.

"Each community can take from the bounty of the earth whatever it needs for subsistence, but it also has the duty to protect the earth and to ensure its fruitfulness for coming generations." (Laudato Si', 67)

Solidarity
The fact that we are all humans connects us in a way that makes us morally responsible for each other.

"The great mistake in regard to the matter now under consideration is to take up with the notion that class is naturally hostile to class, and that the wealthy and the working men are intended by nature to live in mutual conflict. So irrational and so false is this view that the direct contrary is the truth." (Rerum Novarum, 19)

REFERENCES

Leo XIII. Encyclical Letter. *Rerum Novarum.* 15 May 1891

Pius XI. Encyclical Letter. *Quadragesimo Anno.* 15 May 1931

John XXIII. Encyclical Letter. *Mater et Magistra.* 15 May 1961

John XXIII. Encyclical Letter. *Pacem in Terris*. 11 Apr. 1963

Second Vatican Council. Encyclical Letter. *Gaudium et Spes*. 7 Dec. 1965

Paul VI. Encyclical Letter. *Populorum Progressio*. 26 Mar. 1967

Paul VI. Encyclical Letter. *Octogesima Adveniens*. 14 May 1971

John Paul II. Encyclical Letter. *Laborem Exercens*. 14 Sept. 1981

John Paul II. Encyclical Letter. *Sollicitudo Rei Socialis*. 30 Dec. 1987

John Paul II. Encyclical Letter. *Centesimus Annus*. 1 May 1991

Benedict XVI. Encyclical Letter. *Caritas in Veritate*. 29 Jun. 2009.

Francis. Encyclical Letter. *Laudato Si'*. 24 May 2015

Francis. Encyclical Letter. *Fratelli tutti*. 3 Oct. 2020

Made in the USA
Monee, IL
17 November 2021

82364808R00039